GYMNASTICS
UNEVEN PARALLEL BARS

JOANNE MATTERN

The Rourke Corporation, Inc.
Vero Beach, Florida 32964

PROJECT EDITOR:
Genger Thorn is a professional member of USA and AAU gymnastics associations. She is USA safety certified and an associate member of the US Elite Coaches Association (USECA). Genger is currently a girls team coach and director at East Coast Gymnastics, Merritt Island, Florida.

PHOTO CREDITS:
All photos Tony Gray except page 7 © Reuters/Michael Probst/Archive Photos; © Archive Photos/Express Newspapers page 6

EDITORIAL SERVICES:
Janice L. Smith for Penworthy Learning Systems

Library of Congress Cataloging-in-Publication Data

Mattern, Joanne, 1963-
    Gymnastics / by Joanne Mattern
        p. cm.
    Includes bibliographical references and indexes.
    Contents: [1] Training and fitness — [2] The pommel horse and the rings —
[3] The vault — [4] Balance beam and floor exercises — [5] Uneven parallel bars —
[6] Parallel bars and horizontal bar.
    ISBN 0-86593-571-8 (v.1). — ISBN 0-86593-568-8 (v. 2). — ISBN 0-86593-566-1
(v. 3). — ISBN 0-86593-567.X (v. 4). — ISBN 0-86593-569-6 (v. 5). — ISBN 0-86593-
570-X (v. 6)
    1. Gymnastics for children Juvenile literature. [1. Gymnastics.] I. Title
GV464.5.M38 1999
796.44—dc21   99-27924
                                                                        CIP

Printed in the USA

TABLE OF CONTENTS

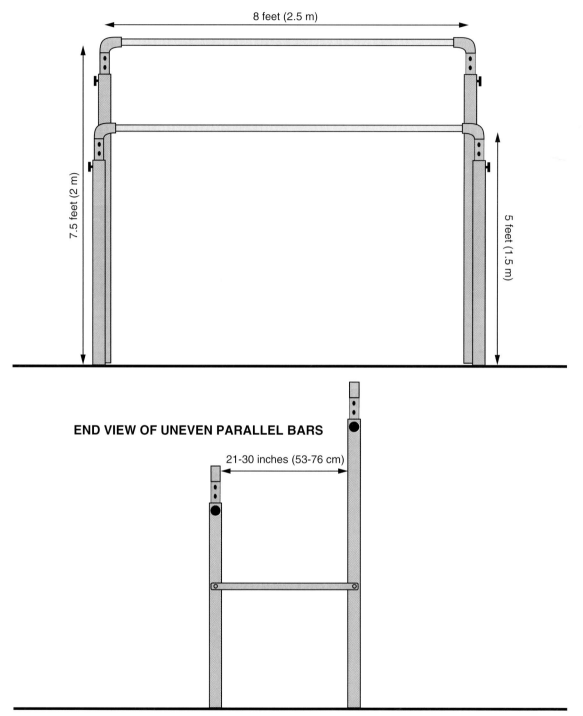

FRONT VIEW OF UNEVEN PARALLEL BARS

8 feet (2.5 m)

7.5 feet (2 m)

5 feet (1.5 m)

END VIEW OF UNEVEN PARALLEL BARS

21-30 inches (53-76 cm)

Dimensions of the uneven parallel bars

GREATEST MOMENTS

The Greatest Moment on the Uneven Bars

For many years, gymnastics has been one of the most exciting events at the Olympic games. During the 1970s, the Russian women's team dominated the sport. The Russians won the major events at the 1972 Olympics and were expected to do the same at the 1976 games in Montreal. Then a tiny Romanian gymnast named Nadia Comaneci entered the arena and captured spectators' hearts.

Nadia was only 14 years old when she came to the 1976 games. She stood just under five feet (1.5 m) tall and weighed just 85 pounds (38 kg). Yet the crowd was spellbound as it watched little Nadia perform daring **routines** (roo TEENZ) that included double backward somersaults and other very difficult stunts.

Nadia didn't just perform difficult routines. She performed them with more confidence, grace, and strength than anyone had ever seen, especially from such a young, small competitor.

Olympic champion Nadia Comaneci

China's Lu Li in her routine, where she scored a perfect 10 and won the gold in 1992

On the first day of the games, Nadia made Olympic history. She performed such a terrific routine on the uneven bars that she received a score of 10.0. That meant that Nadia's routine was absolutely perfect. No gymnast had ever received a perfect score.

The next night, Nadia scored another perfect 10.0 on the uneven bars. She also scored a 10.0 on the balance beam. By the end of the Olympics, she had earned seven perfect scores. Nadia won the all-around championship. She also won gold medals on the uneven bars and the balance beam, along with a bronze medal for the floor exercises and a silver medal for being part of the Romanian team.

Nadia not only made Olympic history, she also inspired many Americans to become involved in gymnastics. Children all over the country were charmed by Nadia and wanted to be like her. Thousands of little girls and boys enrolled in gymnastics schools to learn how to do what Nadia did. Some of these children would grow up to be the Olympic champions of the 1990s.

★ COACH'S CORNER

Scoreboard Confusion

Nadia's first perfect 10.0 on the uneven bars caused some problems for the people running the scoreboard at the Olympics. The electronic scoreboard was not set up to show a score of 10.0, because no one had ever scored so high before. The crowd, and Nadia's coach, were very confused when the scoreboard flashed 1.0 as Nadia's score on the uneven bars. It wasn't until the announcer came on the public address system to say that Nadia had received a perfect score that everyone realized what had happened.

THE EQUIPMENT

The uneven parallel bars is an event for women only. This **apparatus** (AP uh RAT uss), or piece of equipment, was developed from the **parallel bars** (PAIR uh LEL BAHRZ) used by men. During the early 1950s, the height of the bars was changed so that one bar was lower than the other. This created a piece of equipment specially designed for women.

Each bar is about eight feet (2.5 m) long and is attached to uprights mounted on metal or wooden bases. Cables stretch from the bars to the bases to keep the bars from swaying as gymnasts perform on them.

The bars are called "uneven" because one is higher than the other. The high bar is just over seven and one-half feet (just over 2 m). The low bar is just under five feet (1.5 m). In today's competition, slight adjustments in height and the distance between the bars is allowed. The low bar may be between 21 and 30 inches (53 to 76 cm) away from the high bar. This adjustment allows gymnasts of all sizes to use the bars safely.

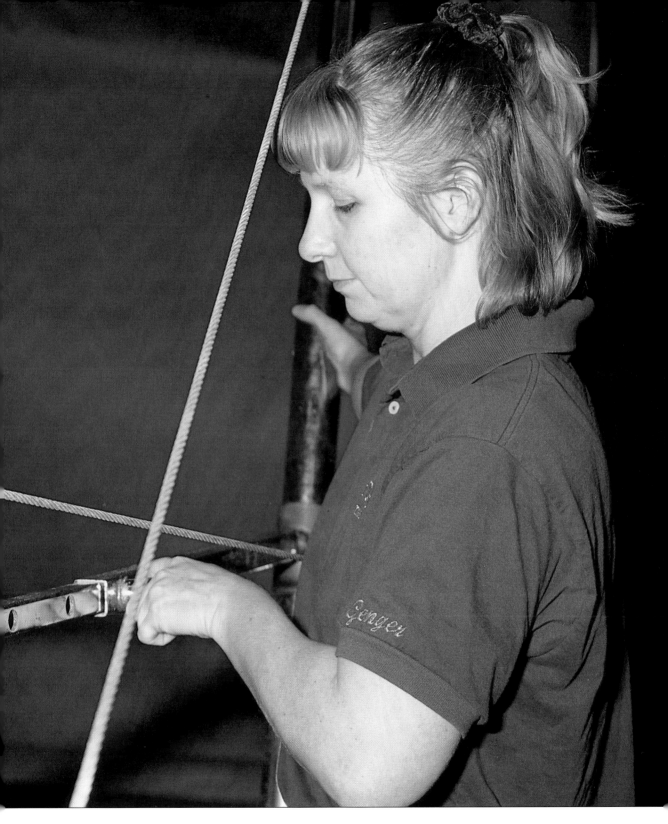

For safety reasons, equipment should be checked before use and the height adjusted for each gymnast.

Uneven bars used to be made of wood, but they often splintered or broke. Today the bars are made of fiberglass covered with a thin layer of wood. The fiberglass makes the bars stronger. It also makes them more flexible to help the gymnast perform turns and flips.

Changing Routines

When the uneven bars were first used in competition, women stood on the low bar in **poses** (POZ ez) and **scales** (SKAYLZ) while holding on to the high bar. Later, gymnasts would hang from the high bar and wrap their hips around the low bar. To allow for this movement, the bars were placed fairly close together.

Today, the bars are placed farther apart so gymnasts can swing from and flip around one bar without hitting the other bar. Many of the skills now used in women's routines were first created by men for the **horizontal bar** (hawr uh ZAHN tul BAHR).

GETTING ON THE BARS

Performing on the uneven parallel bars requires a great deal of upper body strength. Your upper arms, shoulders, back, and abdomen must be powerful enough to support your weight as you pull yourself up, over, and around the bars. Performing strength-building exercises, such as sit-ups and chin-ups, will help you gain the strength you need to succeed in this event. Work with your coach to create an exercise program that fits your needs.

Mounting the Bars

A gymnast may start her routine by mounting the bars from either side. Some basic **mounts** (MOUNTS) are described in this section.

Front-Support Mount

1. Stand facing the low bar with your legs and back straight and your feet together for the front-support mount.
2. Stretch your arms forward and grab the bar in an **overgrip** (O ver GRIP)—fingers curled over the top of the bar.
3. Push yourself up by bending your knees and jumping straight up into the air. At the same time, push down on your hands and straighten your elbows so that you are supporting yourself on straight arms. Your legs should also be straight and stretched back with the toes pointed.
4. Let your weight rest on your upper thighs and hold your head and chest high. Your body should be at a slight angle across the bar.

★ **COACH'S CORNER**

Hips

It's important that you always make contact with the bar where your hips bend. Hitting the bar too far above or below the hips can hurt you.

Getting ready for a front-support mount

Back pullover mount

Back Pullover Mount

For a back pullover mount:

1. Stand facing the low bar with your legs and back straight. Your feet should be together, and your hands should be holding the bar in an overgrip.

2. Pull yourself forward with your arms while you kick your legs high beneath the bar. Kick first with the left leg, then with the right.

3. Hold your legs together and bring them straight up to the far side of the bar. At the same time, pull your body up until you are touching the bar with your hips.

4. Continue pulling until your legs and body pass over the top of the bar. As your feet drop toward the floor, hold your body in the front-support position described on page 14.

★ **DID YOU KNOW?**

Strength Exercises

You need strong abdominal muscles to pull your body into a pike position and send it over the bar. Try hanging from the high bar and pulling your legs up into a tuck. As you gain strength, move from the tuck into the pike. In time, you should be strong enough to move directly into the pike position.

Single-leg Swing-up Mount

The single-leg swing-up mount is another common way to start a routine on the uneven bars.

1. Face and hold the low bar. Then jump up and bring your left (or right) leg into a **tuck** (TUK) position between your arms. Your body should swing beneath the bar while your tucked leg goes over the top of the bar.

2. Whip your right (or left) leg down as you pull yourself up with your arms. These movements will bring your body to the top of the bar. You should end in a **split** (SPLIT) on the bar, supporting yourself on straight arms. Your left (or right) leg will be stretched over the bar toward the front, and your right (or left) leg will be stretched back.

The glide kip mount is the most commonly used to set the gymnast in motion. Kips are the topic of Chapter 5. The glide kip mount is described on page 36.

Performing a single-leg swing-up mount

Single-leg swing-up mount

A gymnast becomes horizontal on the bar so she can perform the front hip circle.

CIRCLING
AND SWINGING

Swinging and circling movements are an important part of a bars routine. Try the simple and advanced moves discussed in this chapter.

Front Hip Circle

1. Start with a front-support mount. Then stretch across the low bar with your body and legs parallel to the floor.

2. Stretch forward to a horizontal position on the bar.
3. Bend at the hips and drop your head and upper body toward the floor until you swing below the bar.
4. Let your hips and legs follow through until you make a complete circle around the bar. Your hands should rotate around the bar as you swing around. End in the front-support position.

Back Hip Circle

Hip circles can also be performed backward. Here's how:
1. Swing your legs back and forth as you hold the front-support position. Then lift your legs high and back as you straighten your arms and push up from the bar. This is called a **cast** (KAST).
2. As your legs reach the bar, curl them underneath it. **Pike** (PIK) your body and let your legs move up on the far side of the bar. Circle the bar with your body and return to the front-support position.

Performing a back hip circle

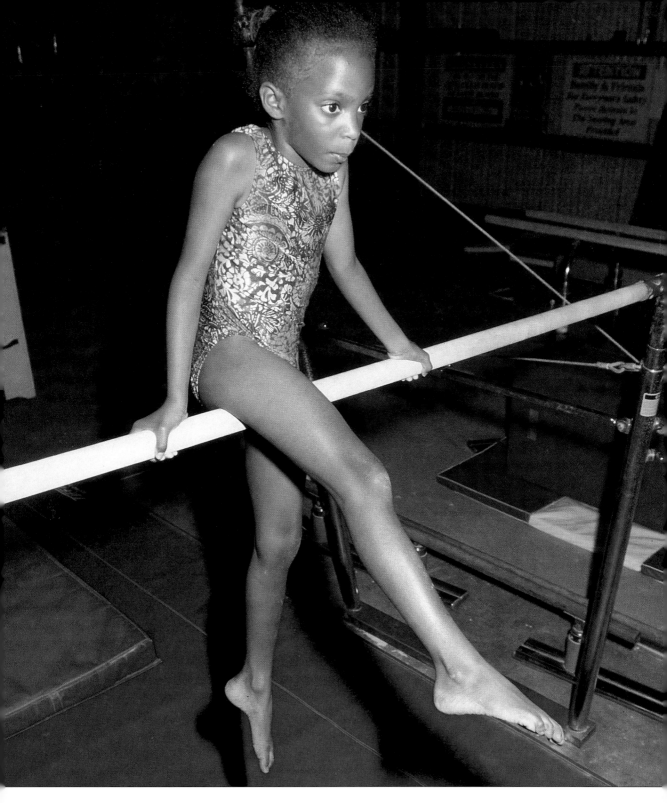

Performing a mill circle forward

Mill Circle Forward

To do a mill circle forward:

1. Start with a single-leg swing-up mount so you are on the bar in a split position. Turn your hands into a **reverse grip** (reh VERSS GRIP)—thumbs pointing toward the front and fingers curled around the back of the bar.

2. Push down on your hands and lift your body up from the bar. Bend your back and bring your chest forward. Your head should be high and your legs should be spread widely apart.

3. Swing your upper body over the bar and toward the floor. The bar should rest against the thigh of your back leg as you swing over it.

4. Rotate your hands around the bar as you circle up to the opposite side. You should end in the original split position.

★ **DID YOU KNOW?**

A Good Arch

The key to a successful mill circle forward is keeping your shoulders back and your chest forward. Your chest must lead the way over the bar if you are to have enough momentum to complete the circle. Keeping your legs straight and your head high will also help you move smoothly and gracefully over the bar.

Clear Hip Circle

A more advanced move is the clear hip circle.

1. Start in the front support position.

2. Perform a cast, or swing, on the high bar.

3. As you return towards the low bar, push down against the bar by extending through the shoulders. Lean backward to initiate the circle around the bar.

4. Push the bar towards your lower thighs while continuing the circle. Keep your body **hollow** (HAHL O), or stretched fully with your back slightly rounded.

5. As your hips rise, pull on the bar, opening your shoulder angle slightly. Shift your hands to the top of the bar to execute a clear hip circle. Return to a support position. Keep your arms straight thoughout the execution.

Finishing a clear hip circle

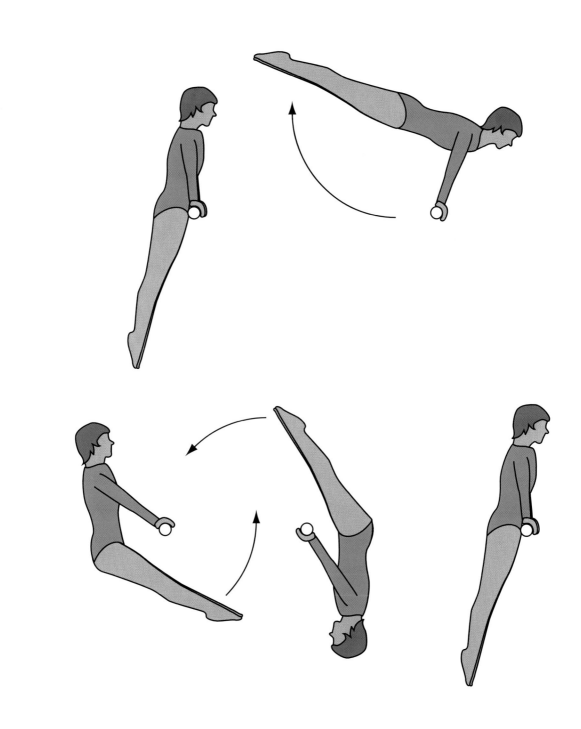

Clear hip circle

Circle Forward

Another advanced move is the circle forward.

1. Stand on the low bar in a pike position with your feet together between your hands. You should be facing away from the high bar. Your hands should be in a reverse grip, and your head should be down.

2. Swing forward and around the bar.

3. As soon as your shoulders rise above the bar, lift your head and look for the high bar.

4. Let go of the low bar and reach up toward the high bar. Be sure to keep your legs pointed straight forward.

5. Lift your legs over the low bar as you grab the high bar in an overgrip.

★ **COACH'S CORNER**

What's in a Name?

Many gymnastics moves are named after the people who invented or perfected them. American gymnast Dominique Dawes has a skill on the uneven bars named after her. A Dawes is a handstand on the high bar, followed by a giant circle backward into another handstand. During the second handstand, the gymnast turns her body one and a half times.

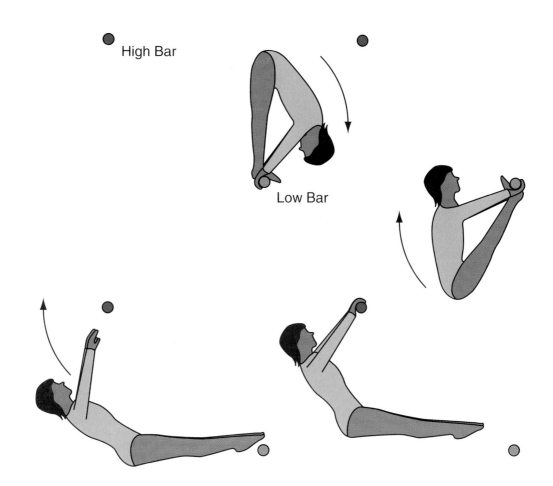

High Bar

Low Bar

Circle forward

Practice with a coach first when attempting new moves.

A Variation on the Circle

You can also perform a variation of the circle forward by following these instructions:

1. Start in the pike position on the low bar while facing toward the high bar.
2. Swing around the bar completely.
3. Jump off of the low bar and grab the high bar.

Swings

Swings are performed as you hang from a bar. You can move all or part way around a bar, or from one bar to the other. Swings are often combined with circles to create exciting moves.

The Cast

The cast is the most basic swing. A cast can be performed on either the high bar or the low bar. To perform a cast on the low bar:

1. Start from the front-support position on the low bar. Bend your hips and swing your legs back and forth beneath the bar.
2. Hold your shoulders over the bar and move your legs high to the rear.
3. Push yourself up so that you are supporting yourself on straight arms. Your body should be hollow—stretched fully with your back slightly rounded—as your legs drop back down to the bar.

To perform a cast on the high bar:

1. Start from a front-support position and swing your legs back and forth.

2. As you reach the top of the backswing, push yourself up and away from the bar. This allows your legs, upper body, and arms to be straight and parallel to the floor.

3. Swing down and beneath the bar into a hanging position.

Under Swing to Counter and Tap Swing

A common swing combination is the under swing to the counter and tap swings.

1. On the high bar in the front support position facing away from the low bar, press the bar downward to the mid to lower thigh. Chest and torso remain hollow and the arms straight.

Performing a cast on the low bar

Swinging from the high bar to the low bar—notice the gymnast is wearing handguards.

2. Swing under and rise upward to execute an under swing.

3. Swing backward toward the low bar, arch slightly under the bar, then hollow out to create the counter swing.

4. Swing forward again, arch right before passing under the high bar and kick your legs forcibly forward.

5. As your hips rise, return to hollow as your toes tap forward to complete the tap swing.

Protecting Your Hands

Working on the uneven bars is very hard on your hands. Constantly rubbing against the bars can cause blisters, scrapes, and cuts. Many gymnasts wear **hand guards** (HAND GAHRDS) until their hands toughen up and form calluses. You can also protect your hands by using gymnastics chalk, working in short sessions, and cupping the bar in your hands rather than gripping it tightly.

Hand guards are used mostly by beginning gymnasts. Once a gymnast becomes more skilled, she uses chalk and grips with dowels to help her hands move smoothly around the bars while circling and swinging.

★ **DID YOU KNOW?**

Practice Each Part

Because the flying hip circle is a difficult move, you should practice each step separately before trying the complete move. First, hang from the high bar and swing into a pike position against the low bar. After you are comfortable with this movement, work on releasing the high bar and grabbing the low bar. Then add the backward hip circle. Be sure to place plenty of mats on the floor below the bars, and always work with a spotter to help you.

KIPPING

A **kip** (KIP) is a crucial move on the uneven bars. A gymnast who can complete kips successfully is able to be competitive at new levels. Types of kips include the glide, long hang, swing, push away, single-leg, and double-leg kip. The glide kip used in levels 4, 5, and 6 of the **compulsory** (kum PAWLSS uh ree) level of competition is the most common.

It is necessary to get your upper body and stomach muscles in peak condition as well as to learn the timing of the kip with your coach.

Double-Leg Stemrise

1. Grab the high bar and rest your feet on the low bar.
2. Push against the low bar with the balls of your feet. Next, straighten your legs until your hips are against the underside of the high bar.
3. Pull free of the low bar by moving your body into a pike.
4. Move into a front-support position on the high bar.

Single-Leg Stemrise

1. Start with your hands holding the high bar and your back across the low bar.
2. Bend your right knee and place your right foot on the low bar. Your left leg should move up to rest on the bar, parallel to the floor.
3. Kick your left leg high. As that leg moves back down, straighten your right leg and move your hips up to the underside of the high bar.
4. Lift both feet away from the low bar and pike your body slightly. End in the front-support position.

Glide Kip Mount

To mount the uneven bars with a glide kip:
1. Jump from both feet, lifting your hips upward and back.
2. Grasp the low bar in the overgrip hand position. Maintain a hollow position with legs extended.
3. Swing forward with legs piked or straddled.
4. After completing the forward swing, close your legs and extend your hips.
5. Quickly lift your feet to the bar and slide your body across the bar from your legs to your hips.
6. Pull downward and shift your hands to the top of the bar to arrive in a front-support position. Your arms should remain straight throughout the move.

A glide kip mount with the legs in a straddle position

What is a Bar Routine?

There is no time limit on a bars routine, but most last 20 to 30 seconds. During this time, an upper level gymnast must move from the low bar to the high bar. She must change her grip and include **release skills** (reh LEESS SKILZ), circles and swings, and changes in direction. A bars routine usually includes 10 to 12 movements. These movements should flow smoothly without any pauses or interruptions. Both bars must be used in level 5 and above, and the gymnast can make no more than five consecutive moves on one bar. Gymnasts at lower levels generally perform on the low bar.

In the 1960s, gymnasts were allowed to stop twice in the middle of a routine on the uneven bars. In the 1970s, they could stop once. Later the rules were changed again. Now gymnasts are not permitted to stop at all during their routine on the bars. They must remain in motion and include at least ten movements in their routine.

What happens if a gymnast falls off the bars during a routine? The judges automatically deduct half a point from her score. But the gymnast is allowed to get back on the bars and finish her routine.

DISMOUNTS

    As with many gymnastics events, a **dismount** (DISS MOUNT) from the uneven bars is very important because it is the last thing the judges see before determining a score. Your dismount should be graceful and smooth. Land on the balls of your feet and bend your knees to absorb the impact. Then drop your heels to the floor and stand at attention with your arms at your sides.

There are more than 21 dismounts for the uneven bars. Three basic dismounts are described in this section.

Cast Off

One commonly used dismount is the cast off.

1. Start from the front-support position. Swing your legs beneath the low bar and then back into a cast.

2. As you reach the top of the cast, push yourself away from the bar.

3. Drop to the floor with your knees slightly bent, then stand in a finished position.

★ **COACH'S CORNER**

Staying Safe

Whenever you work on any gymnastics apparatus, be sure to place floor **mats** (MATS) around the equipment. You should always work with a **spotter** (SPAHT er) nearby to help you and catch you if you fall. It's also important to tie back long hair and to remove any jewelry, such as necklaces or bracelets, that might get caught in the equipment.

Performing a cast off dismount

A coach helps her student work on a difficult dismount.

Flyaway Dismount

The flyaway dismount is a more advanced dismount that should be performed under a coach's supervision.

1. You may start by hanging from the high bar.
2. Swing back and forth until you have good height and speed.
3. When your body has extended and is higher than the high bar, let go of the high bar and flip off in a tuck, pike, or stretch position.
4. Stay until the tuck is complete.
5. Stretch open and land with your knees slightly bent.

Underswing Dismount

For the underswing dismount off the low bar:

1. Start from a front-support position.
2. Initiate a strong cast by shrugging your shoulders towards your ears.
3. Come back to the bars and drop slightly under the bar.
4. Push your toes outward and upward.
5. Stretch and land in a good "stick" position.

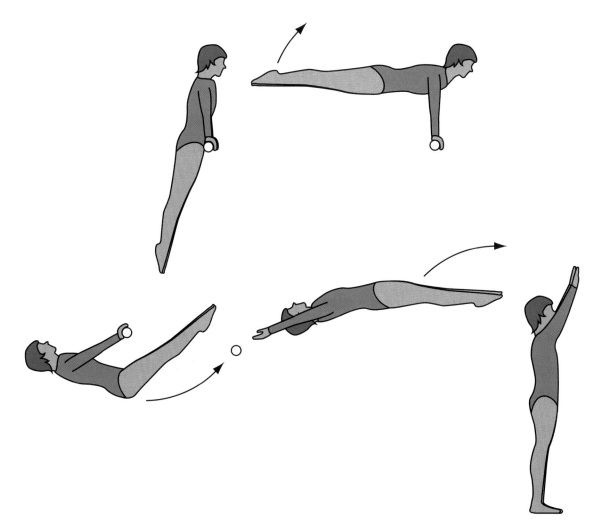

Under swing dismount

GLOSSARY

apparatus (AP uh RAT uss) — a special piece of equipment for performing a gymnastic event

cast (KAST) — the most basic swing used by a gymnast on the uneven bars

compulsory (kum PAWLSS uh ree) — a required routine or movement

dismount (DISS MOUNT) — to get off an apparatus

hand guards (HAND GAHRDZ) — soft leather "gloves" that fit over the middle two fingers and fasten around the wrist to protect the hands

hollow (HAHL O) — a position where the body is stretched fully with a slightly rounded back

horizontal bar (hawr uh ZAHN tul BAHR) — a gymnastics apparatus made of a flexible steel bar that stands about 100 inches (2.5 m) above the floor

kip (KIP) — a movement that takes you from a hanging position into a position where you are supported on your arms

mat (MAT) — a padded surface that provides a soft, safe landing place for a gymnast

mount (MOUNT) — to get on an apparatus

overgrip (O ver GRIP) — holding the bar with your fingers curled over the top

GLOSSARY

parallel bars (PAIR uh LEL BAHRZ) — a gymnastics apparatus made of two bars placed side by side and standing just over five and one-half feet (1.5 m) high

pike (PIK) — a position in which the legs are straight and the body is folded at the waist

pose (POZ) — a position that is held just for a moment

release skills (reh LEESS SKILZ) — skills in which the gymnast lets go of the bar, performs a move, then grabs the bar again

reverse grip (reh VERSS GRIP) — holding the bar with your thumbs pointing toward the front and your fingers curled around the back of the bar

routine (roo TEEN) — a combination of moves displaying a full range of skills

scale (SKAYL) — a balance on one leg

split (SPLIT) — a position in which the legs are held straight and apart

spotter (SPAHT er) — a coach or experienced gymnast who stands below a gymnast to give advice and catch him or her in the event of a fall

tuck (TUK) — a position in which the knees and hips are bent and drawn into the chest

FURTHER READING

Find out more about the uneven parallel bars from these helpful books, magazines, and information sites:

- Feeney, Rik. *Gymnastics: A Guide for Parents and Athletes.* Indianapolis: Masters Press, 1992.
- Gutman, Dan. *Gymnastics.* New York: Viking, 1996.
- Marks, Marjorie. *A Basic Guide to Gymnastics: An Official U.S. Olympic Committee Sports Series.* Glendale, CA: Griffin Publishing, 1998.
- Peszek, Luan. *The Gymnastics Almanac.* Los Angeles: Lowell House, 1998.
- *USA Gymnastics Safety Handbook.* Indianapolis: USA Gymnastics, 1998.

- *USA Gymnastics*—This magazines covers American competitions and athletes, as well as major competitions leading up to the Olympics.
- *Technique*—This publication is geared toward coaches and judges.
- *International Gymnast*—This magazine covers both American and international competitions and athletes.

- www.usa-gymnastics.org
  This is the official Website of USA Gymnastics, the national governing body for gymnastics in the United States.
- www.ngja.org
  National Gymnastics Judges Association, Inc.
- www.ngja.org
  This is the official Website for the National Gymnastics Judges Association, Inc.

INDEX